My First
Picture
Encyclopedia

Contents

Your body

Your bones support your body, and muscles pull the bones to make your body move. Your brain and nerves control your muscles.

X-ray

An X-ray is a kind of photograph that shows your bones.

The bones in your hand fit together like a jigsaw puzzle.

Bones

You have more than 200 bones inside you. They join together to form your skeleton. They get bigger as you grow taller.

Rib cage

As well as supporting your body, your bones protect the soft organs inside you. Your rib cage protects your heart and lungs.

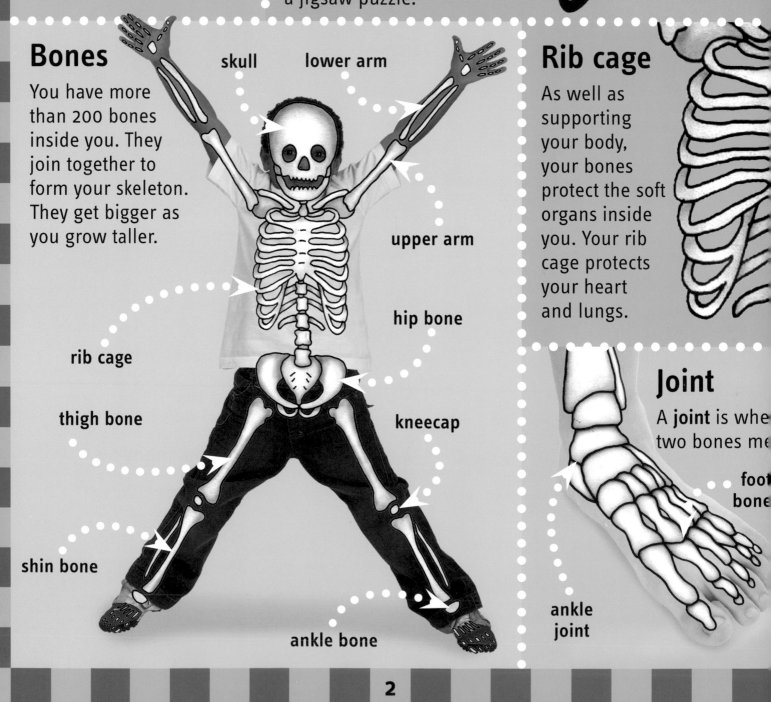

skull

lower arm

upper arm

hip bone

kneecap

rib cage

thigh bone

shin bone

ankle bone

Joint

A **joint** is whe two bones me

foot
bone

ankle
joint

Muscles

Exercising your muscles makes them strong and flexible. You have more than 600 muscles.

biceps muscle

pectoral muscle

thigh muscles

calf muscle

Tendons are like straps. They attach your muscles to your bones.

Brain and nerves

Your brain is small but powerful. You have one and a half times more brain cells than there are people in the whole world! Your brain controls your body. It sends and receives signals along your nerves.

Your brain's wrinkled surface makes it look like a big walnut.

Nerves run down the **spinal cord** in your back

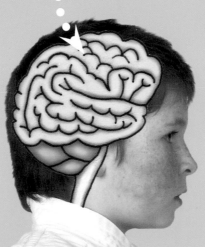

Reflex action

If you touch something sharp like a thorn on a cactus, your nerves make you pull away. This is a reflex action.

Thinking

You also use your brain for thinking, feeling, and remembering.

Heart and lungs

Your lungs take in oxygen from the air. Your heart pumps blood around your body. The blood carries oxygen from your lungs all around your body.

Air enters your **lungs** through air tubes. In your lungs oxygen passes into your blood.

Your **heart** beats without a rest from the moment you are born until the end of your life.

Heart

Your heart is a powerful muscle about as big as your fist. It beats 70 times a minute.

Arteries take blood away from your heart to your body.

Veins carry blood back to your heart.

Asthma

People with asthma sometimes find it hard to breathe. Muscles in the air tubes into their lungs get tight. They take a puff from an inhaler to relax the muscles, and then they can breathe more easily.

Panting

When you run or jump you need more oxygen, so you breathe in and out more quickly.

4

Your digestion

Your body takes the goodness it needs to be healthy out of the food you eat. Your stomach, intestines, liver and kidneys work together every day to do this.

Your **teeth** chew and grind food before you swallow it.

In your **small intestine**, your body absorbs nutrition into your blood.

Your **large intestine** holds the food that your body cannot digest.

Your **stomach** breaks up food into a thick soup.

Your **liver** does almost 500 jobs! The most important is to take food goodness from your blood and send it around your body. It also removes from your blood things that are not good for your body.

Your **kidneys,** which sit behind your intestine, take out liquid waste from your blood and make it into urine (pee).

The waste (poop) leaves your body here.

5

Skin

Your body is covered all over in skin. It is stretchy and tough. It keeps germs and water out and stops you from getting too hot.

Fingerprints

No two people have the same fingerprint. This is the pattern of ridges on the end of your finger.

Cuts

If you fall and cut your skin, your blood cells clot and form a covering or scab over the cut. Then white blood cells attack any germs that might be there. A new layer of skin grows beneath the scab.

Sometimes we put a **bandage** on the cut to protect it.

Skin color

The color of your skin depends on how much dark coloring called melanin you have. Melanin helps prevent sunburn. It blocks out some of the Sun's rays.

Some of us have dark skin.

Some of us have light brown skin.

Some of us have very pale skin.

Sweating

When you are too hot, tiny holes in your skin let out sweat. As the sweat dries, it cools your body down.

Hair

Your hair keeps the Sun's rays from burning your head and helps you stay warm on cold days. Hair also protects your head from bumps and bruises.

Some of us have red hair.

You lose about 90 **hairs** every day! But as long as you stay healthy, more hair grows all the time.

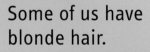

Some of us have tight, curly hair.

Some of us have dark, wavy hair.

Some of us have blonde hair.

Seeing

You see with your eyes. When light enters your eyes, they send nerve messages to your brain to tell it what you are seeing.

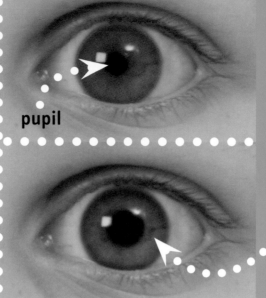

pupil

Pupil

The pupil is an opening in the center of your eye. In the dark the pupil gets bigger to let in more light. On a bright day, the pupil gets smaller to let in less light.

The **iris** is the colored part of your eye.

How you see

Light goes through the **lens** at the front of the eye onto the **retina**.

The image on the retina is **upside down**

A signal goes from the retina to the brain along the **optic nerve**. The brain translates the signal so you see things right side up.

Care for your eyes

Some people need to wear glasses to see clearly. If you need glasses, make sure you wear them.

Hearing

You hear with your ears. The ears respond to sound vibrations in the air. They turn the vibrations into nerve signals and send them to your brain.

Handstand

Nerves like tiny hairs in your inner ear can tell whether you are upside down or right side up.

Sounds we can't hear

Dogs and sea creatures like whales can hear high and low sounds that we can't hear.

How you hear

Your **outer ear** catches sound vibrations in the air.

In your **middle ear** the eardrum vibrates.

From your **inner ear** nerve signals travel to the brain.

"I feel dizzy!"

When you spin around, the nerves in your inner ear send confused messages to your brain. You feel dizzy because you think your head is still spinning even when you have stopped.

9

Tasting

You taste with your tongue. Tiny bumps on your tongue called taste buds respond to different tastes. You have 10,000 taste buds on your tongue!

Bitter

The taste buds on the back of your tongue are sensitive to bitter tastes, like watercress or sprouts.

How you taste

Different parts of your tongue are sensitive to different tastes.

bitter at the back

salty all over

sour at the side

sweet at the front

Salty

Taste buds all over your tongue respond to the flavor of potato chips and other salty foods.

Sweet

You taste sweet foods like frosted cupcakes with the taste buds on the tip of your tongue.

Sour

Sour foods like lemon stimulate the taste buds on the sides of your tongue.

Smelling

You smell with your nose. Hairs at the very top inside of your nose are sensitive to smells in the air. Nerves send signals from your nose to your brain.

How you smell

You suck air onto the sensitive area at the top of your nose to smell something well.

You breathe in through your **nostrils**.

Strawberries smell good.

Blocked nose

Your sense of smell helps you taste things. When you have a cold, and your nose is blocked, you can't taste things very well.

Touching

When you touch things, nerves in your skin send signals to your brain. You can tell if the things are hot or cold, wet or dry, hard or soft, prickly or smooth.

hot

soft

cold

prickly

Plants

People need plants to live. We use plants for food and to make clothes. Plants also release oxygen into the air, and people need oxygen to breathe.

Seeds

Most plants make seeds from which new plants can grow.

Peas are seeds

Spores

Some plants make tiny spores instead of seeds. The spores become new plants.

Moss grows by making spores.

Parts of a plant

Flowers attract insects, birds and other creatures to help make the plant's seeds and fruits.

The **leaves** make sap, the plant's food.

The **stem** supports the other parts of the plant.

To grow, plants need sunlight, water and air.

The **roots** hold the plant in the ground and take in water from the earth.

How plants make food

The leaves absorb the energy in sunlight and use it to make sap (food) from water and a gas called carbon dioxide in the air. As part of this process, the plant releases oxygen.

Chlorophyll (green color) in the leaf absorbs energy.

Birds and insects come to flowers to drink a sweet liquid called **nectar**.

Sticky **pollen** in the flowers attaches to their body or legs.

They carry it to another **flower**.

How plants make seeds

Most plants cannot make seeds on their own. Birds and insects move pollen from one flower to a second one. The second flower uses the pollen to make seeds.

Plants that do not make seeds

Some plants can turn parts of themselves into new plants. A potato is a swollen root of the potato plant. If you don't dig it up, it will turn into a new potato plant.

potatoes

Fruits

Many plants produce fruits, like apples and pears. Inside the fruits are the plant's seeds. Nuts like the walnut and the hazelnut are fruits.

apple

pear

walnut

How seeds grow

A seed splits open and a **root** grows down into the soil.

A green **shoot** grows up from the root.

Trees

Trees have a thick wooden stem called a trunk. They grow tall and get plenty of sunlight. They can live a long time – some redwoods are 2,000 years old!

Blossoms

Some fruit trees grow flowers called blossoms.

Changing colors

Many trees lose their leaves in the fall. Before they fall off, the leaves turn red, orange, or yellow.

How old is it?

You can tell a tree's age by counting the number of rings in the trunk.

Seeds and nuts

Trees grow seeds from whic new trees can grow. In som trees, the seeds are inside nuts.

horse chestnut

swee chest

Bark

The thick outer skin of the tree is called the bark.

Palm trees

Palm trees have thin trunks and large, fringed leaves that we call fronds. Usually palm trees grow in hot places. Coconuts and dates grow on palm trees.

palm frond

Evergreen trees

Some trees stay green all year round. We call them evergreen trees. They usually have needles rather than leaves and grow cones and berries. Evergreens normally grow in cold places. You often see them covered in snow.

Broad-leafed trees

Trees like oaks and beech trees have broad leaves. In the fall, the leaves dry out and fall to the ground. The trees have bare branches in winter before new leaves grow in spring. We also call them deciduous trees.

oak-tree acorn

oak leaf

pine cone

Insects

Most insects have six legs and many have wings. They often use long feelers to smell and touch things. Some insects can taste food using their feet.

Ladybug

black spots

leg

Ants

Ants live together in big groups known as colonies.

Body parts

All insects have three parts to their body. This insect is a beetle.

abdomen

head

thorax

Butterflies

Mother butterflies lay eggs. Caterpillars hatch from the eggs. The caterpillars eat and eat, then cover themselves up. Slowly they change completely and come out as butterflies.

antenna

butterfly

caterpillar

legs

wing

Fly

Bee

Creepy-crawlies

Are snails and millipedes insects? Do they have six legs? Do they have three parts to their body?

snail

millipede

Spiders are not insects. They have eight legs, not six.

Birds

Birds are the only animals that have feathers. There are thousands of types of birds. They live all over the world. All birds have wings, but not all birds can fly.

Ostrich

Ostriches can run very fast but they cannot fly.

long legs

Penguin

Penguins live in freezing Antarctica. They can't fly but they use their wings for swimming.

Eagle

wide wings

talons or claws

A nest of eggs

Baby birds hatch from **eggs**.

Owl

Owls have large eyes and very good hearing. They hunt at night.

Duck

waterproof feathers

Parrot

Parrots live in the trees of the rain forest.

Pets

We keep pet animals at home. Hamsters live in cages, and puppies have baskets. Rabbits and tortoises need to live in your garden or yard.

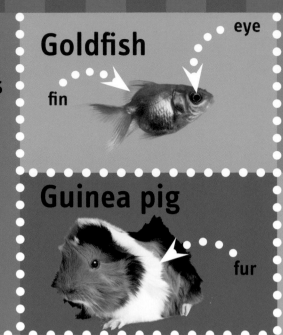

Goldfish

eye

fin

Budgie

perch

tail feather

Guinea pig

fur

Hamster

Hamsters run on a wheel in their cage.

Kitten

whiskers

ear

Tortoise

Always wash your hands after handling your tortoise. Some tortoises can live to be 100 years old.

hard shell

Puppy

You need to train your puppy. This means teaching it to behave well. You can start training it when it is about four months old.

Rabbit

Rabbits have long ears. They like eating grass and other plants.

Farm animals

All these animals live on the farm. The farmer gets up early every day to milk the cows, and to make sure that the other animals are safe and well fed.

Horse

Horses are strong. They pull the farmer's cart.

Chicks

fluffy feathers

beak

Goose

webbed feet

long neck

Pig

To keep cool, pigs roll in mud. A pig will eat almost anything. He sniffs out food with his snout.

snout

Goat

Farmers make delicious cheese from goats' milk.

Sheep

People make wool from a sheep's coat.

Rooster

Cock-a-doodle-do! The call of a rooster wakes up the farmyard in the morning.

Cow

Some farmers keep cows for their milk.

Wild animals

Animals in the wild need to be strong and alert. They have to find their own food. Sometimes they have to fight with or run away from other animals.

Lion

mane

Lions can eat 75 lbs (34kg) of meat in one meal - that's the same as 300 quarter-pound hamburgers!

tail

Zebra

Zebras are white with black stripes.

Bear

long shaggy fur

strong back leg

sharp claws

Cheetah

A cheetah can run three times as fast as the quickest Olympic athlete.

spotted coat

Monkey

baby

Most monkeys live in trees. They are great at jumping and climbing!

long arm

Elephant

large ear

Elephants have huge ears and very good hearing. They live in jungles or grasslands.

tail

trunk

Giraffe

bony horn

Giraffes are tall enough to eat leaves at the very top of tall trees.

Sea animals

In the ocean, beautifully colored fish live among sharks, squid, and other sea creatures. Many feed on underwater plants. Others are hunters.

Jellyfish

Jellyfish have no heart, no blood, and no brain!

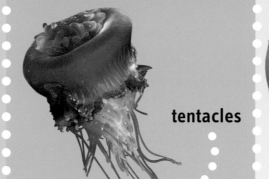

tentacles

Stingray

Stingrays have poisonous **spines** in their tail.

eye

Sea turtle

Sea turtles can live for up to 80 years.

flipper

shell

head

Starfish

Starfish live on the sea floor.

Tropical fish

percula clown fish

regal fish

Shark

Sharks have several rows of teeth. New teeth are growing all the time.

eye

dorsal (back) fin

tail fin

snout

fin

coral

butterfly fish

In space

The Earth is one of eight planets that travel through space around the Sun. The Sun and the eight planets make up the solar system.

Day and night

The Sun shines on half the Earth at any one time. When it shines on the part where you are, it is day. When it is day on your half of the Earth, it is night on the other half.

day   night

Earth and its moon

The Earth spins as it goes around the Sun. It takes 24 hours (one day and one night) to spin around once.

moon

Sun

Earth

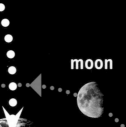

Earth's moon

When sunlight hits all of the moon's face that we see from Earth, we call it a **full moon**.

The moon travels around the Earth. It reflects the Sun's light. The moon takes more than 27 days to travel round the Earth.

The solar system

Neptune
Uranus
Saturn
Jupiter
Mars
Earth
Venus
Mercury
Sun

Galaxies

Our Sun is just one of thousands of stars. Groups of stars are called galaxies. The galaxy we live in is called the Milky Way. Galaxies come in different shapes. Spiral galaxies have curving arms.

Stars in the night sky

If you live in the southern half of the Earth, you can see the **southern cross**.

If you live in the northern half of the Earth, you can see the **plow**.

Sometimes we see a **half moon**, when the Sun lights up only half of the surface that is facing Earth.

When the part of the moon lit by sunlight faces mainly away from Earth, we see a **crescent moon**.

We can use a **telescope** to look at the stars.

Continents and oceans

The world contains seven continents or large blocks of land. The seven continents cover only one-third of the world's surface. The rest is ocean.

Europe

Europe contains the beautiful city of Paris, in France.

Eiffel Tower, Paris

Africa

Africa contains the world's biggest desert - the Sahara.

sand dunes in the Sahara Desert

North America

Canada, Mexico and the United States are all part of North America.

skyscrapers in New York City

South America

South America contains the vast Amazon rain forest.

tree frog

North America

Europe

Pacific Ocean

Atlantic Ocean

South America

Africa

Antarctica

Asia

China is in Asia. More people live in China than in any other country in the world.

The Great Wall of China

Oceans

There are five main oceans - the Pacific, the Atlantic, the Indian, the Arctic, and the Southern Oceans. The Pacific is the largest of these.

dolphins playing in the Pacific Ocean

Arctic Ocean

Asia

Pacific Ocean

Indian Ocean

Southern Ocean

Australia and Oceania

Australia and Oceania

Australia, New Zealand and many Pacific islands are part of this continent.

Uluru, Australia

Antarctica

Almost the whole continent of Antarctica is covered with thick ice.

seal in Antarctica

Volcanoes

A volcano is a hole in the Earth's surface. When hot liquid rock spills out through the hole, we say the volcano is erupting. The liquid rock is called lava.

Fertile land

The land near volcanoes is usually very good for growing food.

flames

smoke

volcano crater

flow of lava

What's inside

The top layer of the Earth's surface is the **crust**. Beneath the hard crust is liquid **molten rock**. In the center is the **solid core**.

solid core

crust

molten rock

Earthquakes

The Earth's crust has split into large pieces called plates. When they move, they cause an earthquake. In a large earthquake, roads crumble and buildings fall down.

Tsunamis

An earthquake under the sea can create a giant wave called a tsunami. When it hits land, a tsunami can cause terrible damage.

Landslides

In a landslide, rocks and earth come loose and fall down the side of a mountain or hill. Landslides are caused by earthquakes, and sometimes also by floods from overflowing rivers or heavy rainfall.

crack in road

Religions

Many people have a religion. They worship a god or gods, and follow teachings on how to live. Each religion has its own holy books.

Christianity

Christians worship one God. At Christmas they celebrate the birth of God's son, Jesus Christ, who lived on Earth 2,000 years ago. They worship in a church.

Islam

Muslims worship one God, Allah. They follow the teachings of the prophet Mohammed, who lived on Earth 1,400 years ago. Their religion is called Islam. They are taught to pray five times every day.

Buddhism

Buddhists follow the teachings of an Indian princ the Buddha, who lived on Earth 2,500 years ago. They worship in a temple. Some Buddhists like to hang praye flags outside their homes.

Statue of the **Buddha**

The Christians' holy book is the **Bible**.

My First Bedtime BIBLE

The Muslims' holy book is the **Koran**.

Hinduism

Hindus worship many gods and goddesses. They usually see them as different forms of one God. Their holy books are called the Vedas. Some Hindus believe that God is in everything that exists.

Hindus worship at home or in a temple called a **mandir**.

Statues of gods and godesses.

khism

hs worship one God. ey follow the teachings ten gurus or teachers. e first was Guru Nanak, o lived in India about 0 years ago. Sikhs worship d by meditating on his me, Waheguru.

Sikh men and boys wear a **turban**.

Judaism

Jews worship God in a synagogue. Their religion is Judaism. In many of their festivals - like Pesach (Passover) each spring - they remember important events in their long history.

The Jewish holy book is the **Torah**. Jews read from it in the synagogue.

Travelers and explorers

In the past many explorers went on great journeys to find new lands. Today travelers take difficult trips because they want adventure.

Poles

American explorer Robert Peary led the first trip to reach the North Pole, in 1909. Roald Amundsen of Norway was the first man to reach the South Pole, in 1911.

Skis make it easier to travel over snow.

Moon landing

On 21 July 1969, American astronaut Neil Armstrong became the first man to walk on our moon. He flew there on the Apollo 11 spacecraft.

The United States flag

Armstrong left footprints on the moon's surface.

Australia

Aborigines have lived in Australia for 30,000 years. The first Europeans discovered Australia in the 1700s.

Vikings

About 1,000 years ago Vikin from Norway, Sweden, and Denmark seized land all ove northern Europe. They were fierce fighters, who sailed ir longships.

The highest mountain

In 1953, Edmund Hillary and Tenzing Norgay were the first people to climb Mount Everest. Everest is 29,035 feet (8,850 meters) tall - the world's highest mountain. It is right on the border between Nepal and Tibet.

Pacific Islanders

About 30,000 years ago, people from Asia began to explore the islands in the Pacific Ocean. They sailed a very long way in light canoes. Today their descendants - the Pacific Islanders - live on thousands of islands in the Pacific Ocean.

Camels can carry people or bags of goods.

From Italy to China by camel

Italian merchant Marco Polo traveled across land, mainly by camel, from Italy to China in 1271-75. He wrote a book, **The Travels of Marco Polo**, to tell Europeans about life in Asia.

Discovering America

In 1492, Italian sailor Christopher Colombus tried to sail to Asia from Europe by going west instead of east. He discovered America!

INDEX

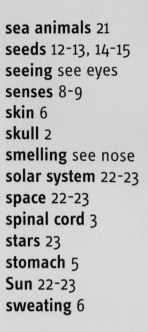